SELF PORTRAIT

Barbara Elizabeth Mercer

SELF PORTRAIT

Barbara Elizabeth Mercer

Cyberwit.net
HIG 45, KAUSHAMBI KUNJ, KALINDIPURAM,
ALLAHABAD - 211011 (U.P.)
India

Tel. (91) 9415091004
E-mail: cyberwit@rediffmail.com
www.cyberwit.net

ISBN 81-8253-065-2
First Edition: 2006
Rs. 120/-

Cover Painting
Self Portrait

Title: Our Lady Of Dreams

Artist: Barbara Elizabeth Mercer, CPA (Canadian Portrait Academy)

Date: 2003

Medium: Acrylic on Gallery Canvas

Size: 24 x 24

From the Series – My Canadian Icons, Those Who Have Influenced My Life
Nine Portraits In the Shape of a Canadian Diamond Canadian Representative

The 2003 Invitational

Biennale Internatazionale Dell'Arte Contemporanea
Citta di
Firenze
Florence, Italy

Printed in India at Astha Associates, Allahbad

Dedication

For Andrew and Renu
More Than I Can
Express

Love

Loyalty

Friendship

Forever

Foreword by Maria Cristina Azcona

Barbara Mercer's book of poetry may be considered a perfect ensemble of the reflection of her own livable experiences and her aesthetic sensibility, as a painter who at the same time, is a poetess. The book is an artistic self-biography where all the awesome skills of the author conforms an *aquarelle* of incredible value around her own life remembrances.

The poems flow sweetly, naturally, in front of the reader eyes, exposing her story to several levels of interpretation. Visually, melodiously, conceptually, we roam through the sidewalks and paths of her own personality that is present all the time in her constructions.

We are able to live her memories through this narration, and through that description, since she wants us to enter this journey, deliberately. She recreates the scenes and the sensations that marked her destiny, intending us to understand, to comprehend why she became a painter and a poetess. We can include her magnificent work in postmodern poetry, because it develops all the characteristics of this style.

In this sense, we find a particular way of cutting the edges of the verses.

The February
storm

She uses alliterations (in this case T) and redundancies of words, that are full of sense, like "fate".

Fate has a timing
Adjust to the time

Furthermore, we may enumerate also the description of reality from a conceptual point of view that includes a subliminal ecological critic.

Sawdust is flying
Smog
persisting

In fourth place, we find the inner rhythm, which is a musical constant in her poetry.

A jig is being jigged

Barbara is a consecrated painter, and this particularity creates in her poetry, a visual kaleidoscope of colors and shapes, of incredible beauty, where music is not absent from the landscape of her life, brilliant under the rainbow, which is her palette of colors.

Today it is mine
Red! Red! Red!

Her verses are full of meanings, sensations, images and metaphors, in a wonderful synthesis, the poem itself. As a reader, I loved in her verses the perfect harmony among rhythm, colors, comparisons and visual images. She is able to manage timing of each particular syllable, and its conjunction in the group of words, into the line. This author shows an experienced hand when she writes the poem in apparently casual sequences that are truly born in her soul and will. She gains the attention as a talented poetess who is owner of our more distinguished respect.

I am deeply convinced that Poetry is the language of spirituality, the verbal tool of angels and the inspiration of lovers. A good poem is a beautiful pond where profound meanings float like petals. Sometimes, the conglomerate of words is a not an owner of mysterious beauty, a small fairy who escapes from the hand of many poets. In contrary, in her book, the most exigent reader of poetry will be able to enjoy the melodious sounds that surge like an audible stream in each poetical scheme. While reading, you will enter an enchanting world full of richness: Barbara Mercer's life itself, visible, audible, enjoyable, without pause, restless. A life story of a true artist.

María Cristina Azcona

María Cristina Azcona is an internationally published writer and bilingual poetess born in Argentina, who is also Editorial Advisor to the *Taj Mahal Review*. She is a Peace Literature expert to the encyclopedia EOLSS (UK). Her poems and literary articles can be read in many magazines and newspapers around US, UK, Brazil, Jordan, India and her own country. She has authored a novel, an essay and three books of poems, including the poetry collection *Window to Heaven*, also published by Cyberwit.net.

Acknowledgments

First and foremost, to Karunesh Kumar Agrawal, Deputy Managing Editor, Cyberwit.net, for his continued help, patience and guidance in this my second book of poetry. And to Argentina's Maria Cristina Azcona, writer, bilingual poetess, Editorial Advisor to the Taj Mahal Review, Peace Literature expert to the encyclopedia EOLSS (UK), for generously writing the review, Forword. For her truly deep understanding of what my poetry is saying. She leaves me speechless and humbled, I am honoured and eternally grateful.

I cannot fully express my gratitude to all those who have helped me, in so many ways to complete this book.

Thank you especially to my son, Andrew Judd, Artist, Art Director, for his expert advice, constant enthusiasm and support in helping me choose the cover. Dear and trusted friends, Stephen Ford, Financial advisor, Cathy, and children Austin and Jasmine, my godchild, for their friendship, support and inspiration. Special friend, Author, Historian, Prof. Emeritus, Trevor O. Lloyd, whose wit, understanding and humour, lightened my journey into the mysterious world of poetry publishing. Sr. Eduardo Robson, Vicepresidente, Merrill Lynch International, Latin America, youthful sparring partner, for the Mexican experience and helping me to remember through expressing my poetry with the gift of music. Trusted friend, Liz Wylie, Curator, University of Toronto Art Centre, for her continued optimism, inspiration and humour. Fellow members and colleagues, The Arts and Letters Club of Toronto, Knights in shining armor, Keron Platt, Gary Stark and Lady Flora Danziger, who came to my aid on the occasion of my first book of poetry Mystic Wills launch, 2005. Dear friend, Mrs. Sharon Cunningham, for her belief and support, during the illness of her husband Len. Journalists, Justin Skinner, Lorriana De Giorgio, Catherine Tammaro, for their dedication and newspaper articles.

To Martin Lortz, Photographer, Web Designer, for front cover photograph. Farid Kayali, Computer Technician, Sophie Sudano, Photographer, for the exceptional and amazing back cover photograph.

Finally, I would be remiss if I did not mention the two most extraordinary people who have touched my life so deeply, and inspired the flow of words, my son Andrew Judd and daughter-in-law Renu Sarao whose combined inspiration, encouragement, excitement, creativity and leadership, are a constant reminder of worlds we will travel in exploration without exception.

Waves of love to all......

The Author

Author of MYSTIC WILLS
Selected Poems, Cyberwit.net,
2005

SELF PORTRAIT is Mercer's 2nd book of Poetry.

Barbara Elizabeth Mercer, CPA, (Canadian Portrait Academy) poet, painter, born Galt/Cambridge, Ontario, Canada. Subsequent studies: New York, San Francisco, Cal., Toronto, On, Canada, where she worked with educational TVOntario, The Canadian Broadcasting Corp., The Canadian Opera Co., The National Ballet of Canada and other theatre groups. Although her main focus has been painting, she has been writing poetry for many years.

As a member of the prestigious Arts and Letters Club of Toronto, made her poetical/performing debut in 2004 and as a member of The Canadian Poetry Association, was published in the 2005, 20th Anniversary publication, Poemata. Member of The Ontario Poetry Society, published in Verse Afire, 2006 and Enchanted Crossroads anthology, 2006.

Mercer's publications include Cyberwit.net anthologies: Harvests of New Millennium, (Two Paintings), First Edition 2006, Explorers 2005, New Pegasus 2004, Taj Mahal Review, December 2004. Symphonies 2003. Three US Anthologies. Fledgling Press, Edinborough, Scotland.

Barbara Elizabeth Mercer's paintings are included in the permanent collections of The University of Toronto Art Centre, Imperial Oil, The Robert McLaughlin Gallery, as well as many international private collections.

EXHIBITIONS 2006: Finalist, International Itinerant Digital Exhibition M.I.A.D. Venado Tuerto, Argentina.

Barbara lives in Toronto, On CANADA,

Website: www.barbaraemercer.com

Contents

COLOUR

You have many colours
Spread neatly
On your palette
North light in your windows
Brushes in your
Hand
Through country landscape
Your blue eyes find a lover
Now winter holds
You
Thoughts fly over rooftops
Rooms filled with fragrance
Wood burning in
The hearth
Moonbeams
Crystal snow flakes
Diamonds
Painted air with
Magic
Nose pressed on windows
Finding colour everywhere
Rainbow's
Spectrum
Glistening window panes
Colour splashed reflecting
Through beveled glass
Doors
Mirrors sparkling answer dancing
Colour painting my world
Colour
Everywhere

CHAIN BRACELET

The gift
A Mexican silver
Bracelet
Thickness
Of soft smooth
Rolling Chain
Encircled my wrist
Clasped with a
Toggle of gold
A gift of love
Representing our entwined lives
Years had
Passed
Since our youth
Many loves
Broken chains
Put aside
Never
Repaired
This Mexican chain
Endures - binds - caresses
Memories
Interlocking
Insists on returning
Then enfolding
Into itself
Weighted
By
Fullness

BETWEEN REVELATION

Between revelation
Open
Silence
Open heart
Present thoughts
Remaining fingers
Focused desire
Tipped
With love

ANOTHER WAVE PROPAGATION

Do we know
With what
Seed - pebble
What wave we have evoked
By a thought
By an
Action
Innocent
Malignant
Loving
Controlling
Hateful
Jealous
Envious
Grateful
Thankful
Mournful
Prayerful
Pleasure
-Desperate
Erotic - longing
Satisfied - needy
What magnetism
Travels
In the wind
Through sun dappled gardens
Roof tops
Singing fountains

HOUSE HOME CASTLE

December 13, 2005
Well
house I am yours
You are mine and CHIPS and Empire Insurance
Life Annuity
I
Can now love you for as long as I live
In you - you live through
Me
They could erect a plaque on our front lawn
Mystic Poet Of Cabbagetown
1933 -
In a hundred years after I am gone
I will live with your
Imperfections - try not to let you crumble
Maintain your Victorian stature
Proud
To stand at the south corner of Pine Terrace
An anchor for this ship of
Row houses built 1886
In Cabbagetown
Toronto Ontario Canada
Your grand
East west wings
Will hold me with strength - beauty -
History
Creativity - adventure
With guard goddess cat Frigga
With my paintings covering

Your walls
With my first book of poetry
MYSTIC WILLS
With millennium
Swedish Jotul wood burning stove
You are my refuge
My house - home -
Castle

CROW AND FALCON

Black crow crowns top of
Tallest tree
Bobbing back and forth
Calling to me
Pay attention to what I
Say
What is it you want me to see
Crows beak points down to lower
Branch
Still tall in tree
A falcon sits
Majestically - silently
Head turning
Slowly
Displaying his golden eye to me
He is the peregrine
Falcon
Proudly surveying his domain
As ancient Egypt
The all seeing eye of king
Horace
Brings message from other world
What is your message for me
On
Greatest spreading wings
Slowly takes flight toward eastern light into
Night
Crow follows
Led by golden thread held in his beak
Peregrine falcon
The golden trail
Where will it lead
What is your message for me

CRY OF THE PEREGRINE FALCON

4:47 A.M.
Awakened by
Loud noises
Thumping scrambling
On the roof above
Her sleeping
Bed
Then the loud whistle cry
Of
The Peregrine Falcon
A celebratory
Cry
Triumphant cry
The prey subdued
In the talons
Of
The Peregrine Falcon
The
Swift descent
The unsuspecting prey
The golden eye of Horace
The shape
Shifter of ancient Egypt
Then stillness of darkest night
She had heard
Only the cry
Of the Peregrine Falcon

CRESCENT CREAM MOON

August 10, 2005
Quarter
Crescent cream moon
Appears in slightly blue sky
After rain showers
Thunder
Pink voluminous clouds
More slowly into deep gray
Then into night
Sky
To the east
Good evening
Mr. crescent cream moon
Reflection in pools of
Rain
On terraces, rooves, sidewalks
Parking lots
In this great city
Good
Evening
Mr. crescent cream moon
Fragrance of freshness
Embraces this
Great city
Refreshes
After searing heat
Good evening
Mr. crescent cream
Moon

A THOUGHT

Through sun dappled
Gardens
Rooftops
Singing fountains
Traffic
Congested roads
Row houses
Thoughts
Emanate
Through connecting beams
Through walled back yards
Open terraces
Front
Gated entrances
Through fragrant cigar smoke
Through tight lips
Through
Dishonest subterfuge
Through desire to be on top
Bigger - larger - real
Estate
Our wave thoughts
Swirls into a hurricane
Of destruction
Or of
Love
Or
Our particular
Wave
Of
Thought

DAWN

Dawn spilling gold
Over silhouetted tree tops
Shimmering
Roof tops - pools of rain
Terrace boards - railings - stairs
Furled
Umbrellas
Dispersing fog
Gathered on spires of Bay Street
5:47 - 6:47 -
7:00 A.M.
Wet nose to nose kiss
From Frigga cat
Wake up - wake
Up
Traffic begins moving
Journey humming
Sirens screaming
Through streets
Globe
And Mail hits door
Raccoons walking their high wire highway
Planes
Leaving trails
Leaving Pearson International
My world awakens
In
Cabbagetown
Lacy rippled shadows

ART WEAVING

Confined in my country
I send
Threads of weaving
Through the miracle
Of internet communication
Forming a
Web of hope
In foreign countries
Through digital communication
Artists
Are weaving
Beyond borders
Beyond politics
Beyond restrictions
Beyond the
Preconceived
Encircling the globe
We are weaving
Delicate
Golden
Threads of communication
Where we have not the means
To Financially
Appear
We explore the spiritual universe
Touching hearts
In our cosmos
Of Art
Weaving

DANCING

After the movie
Secret Of The Black
Pearl
In Mexico City
At his Casa Grande
He played wonderful music
She drank
Wine
She danced for him
While he encouraged
Her to continue
His
Expression in awe
His blue eyes
Amazed
She danced freely
To the rhythms
You
Promised me
You would dance with me
He stood approached her
Slowly
Deliberately
Fixing her with his eyes
Their bodies touched
She was willing
To be led
He was gentle - formal
They moved to the rhythm
Softly -

Slowly - gently
Magic of Latin music
They
Floated
For an instant
A moment in time
Dancing in Mexico City
He stood
Proud
On his territory
He stood with a lifetime
Of experience -
Memories
He stood elegant - formal
Respectfully as a frame
Ready to receive
Her
Into his arms
She entered - confident
Feeling the rhythm - the
Music
Of time
For a moment
Synchronized by the stars
Which brought them
Together
So many years ago
And so they danced
On his territory
In his Casa
Grande
In Mexico City
Dancing their lives away

DEEPEST EMOTION

Deepest emotion
Souls
Unstifled
Opening genius
Arpeggios
Greatest key
Master secret
Innocent
Consent
Diminishing sorrow
Deepest Emotion

ENTERTAINER

A jig is being jigged
On my lighthouse
roof
A tango is being tangoed
On my lighthouse roof
A tarantella is being
Performed
On my lighthouse roof
A tap dance is being tapped
On my
Lighthouse roof
A marathon is being run
On my lighthouse roof
There is an
Entertainer
On my lighthouse
Roof
Vying for attention
On my lighthouse roof
Black beady sparkly eyes
Looking for an audience
On my lighthouse
Roof
Bushy tail flailing about
On my lighthouse roof
There is a cheeky
Little face
Looking through the skylight
On my lighthouse roof
It is
The entertainer
I shall go down and find some food
To. feed the
Entertainer

ETERNAL BEAUTY

For: Renu Sarao

Upon meeting
The amazing
Beauty
Of my long lost
Then found
Daughter-in-law
Quietly - strength
Recognized
I approached with hesitancy
Not knowing
How I had been - or
Would be
Perceived
Dark shining eyes smiling
Held acceptance
It would take
Time
It would take love - courage
Andrew Judd - my son
Who
Circumstances forced me
To give away at birth
And with
Renu's strength - helped
And encouraged
In searching for me
Until I was found
My daughter-in-law
Is
Eternal beauty

EXQUISITE KNOWING

Knowing the agony
Of a lover's
Longing
Turmoil his life
Searching for answers
Asking for
Recognition
Needing to share
Ashamed to reveal his trouble
Wanting to respond
I know
The agony
Exquisite knowing
Not privileged to enter
Between his
Trouble
His life was once sweet
Innocent troubled loving
Exquisite long
Distance loving
Exquisite Knowing

FATE

Fate has a timing
Adjust to the time
Be
Ready for
The unexpected
Will of Fate
Be still
Be creative
Be
Listening
For the secret blessings
Of Fate
Move forward
With respect -
Humility
Learn to love
Fate
A higher power
Will Shower
With what we need
Fate
At
It's own speed

FATE MAP

I have heard

If you draw a map

Of everywhere you

Have been

You draw your fate

Can this be true?

Shall I dare to draw

The

Map?

Can I remember

Everywhere I have been?

What is the next point

Next intersection on the road

To The Map of my fate

Dare to draw

Foretell

My fate

Is it a circle

Surrounding me

Forward - forward

Until it

Is

Return - return

A mandala

To the centre

The starting point of The Map

Of

My fate?

Draw

FEBRUARY FULL MOON

Brightest February Full
Moon
Encircled by mist
Glows the world beneath
Crystal sparkles the world
Beneath
Through sky windows
Grazed with diamonds
Thrown by a heavenly
Moonbeam hand
Mysterious message
Do not neglect me
Written with
Sureness
Written in italic script
With iridescent ink
Flowing smoothly
On
Slippery frozen glass
Swirled with diamonds
February Full Moon

FEBRUARY STORM

She lay beneath
The February
Storm
Beneath the grand duvet
Warm comforted safe
Watching lightning
Dance
Ceiling walls
Flash through mirrors
Listening to heavy raindrops
On
Skylight glass roof
A million rushing feet
Landing with force
Her tower
Of light tonight
Loving the sounds sights
The music of February
Storm
And thought of him
Of the music of love
He sent to her from far away
Then
Listened together long distance
How like their love
Is this
February
Storm

FEBRUARY SUNRISE

Cold frost sparkled
Morning
Breathing life into day
Sun rises pink, gold, triumphant
Over this
Victorian Enclave
Named Old Cabbagetown
In the centre of this great city
Red
Brick houses standing tall
As history
Topped with snow, crystal
Chandeliers
After midnight storm fiercely swirling
Windows gaze out
On
Shimmering spires
Reflecting gold, silver, bronze
Bay Street's commerce
Giants
Decks, terraces, high with pink, gold smiling snow
Snow rising white,
Blue, violet clouds
Trees silhouettes greeting
Birds high flying
Flight
Then pure blinding gold of
February Sunrise

FIRST LOVE

You were 26
I was 16
We smiled
Shyly through noise of presses
Churning out
Newspapers
In a small
River
Valley town
You were tall - golden
I was young - intimidated
You were
Graduated
I had not begun
You were worldly
I was lacking in
Worldliness
You were on the road
To greatness
I had not yet begun
I would see
Glimpses of you
In headlines
You showed me fine paintings
I doubt if you ever
Saw glimpses of me
In headlines
I do not know if you ever knew
I so
Admired you
You - my first love

FLAMES

In and out of memory
In and out of
Dreams
Faces return - fade - return - fade
Words of love encircle
Hazy - cloudy
- drifting - wafting
In and out of memory
Blue eyes closely
Inquiring
Are you still there - alive
Do you remember me
If you come back
Will I
Recognize you
Will you know me
Will I make you laugh
Will I make you
Dance
Will you still like me
You have had many wives
I have had many
Lovers
Will you still ask my forgiveness
Will I still accept - forgive
The
Clearer memories
Of my old flames

FRAMES

Frames of Mexican silver
Reflecting
Light curved and smooth
Swirls in four corners
A Labyrinth
Frame of black
Leather stitched in beige
Frames framing photographs
Frames of how we
Were not so long ago
Frame encloses a beautiful boy
Frame encloses the
Impresario
Reminding of our first meeting
Frame encloses two of us
Our
Meeting - friendship renewed after 43 years
To remind of three years
Ago
In Mexico against a stone wall
Looking out from a lookout
Far above a
Verdant valley
Frame black leather
Impresario smiling in his tower
On
The seaside of Miami
Dragon sculpture guarding
Red gift bag displaying

Birthday celebration

Frames standing guardians

Our past receding

Fast

Stand firm on my desk framing my journal of

Things to do events to

Remember

Our life of Frames

FULL MOON

Brightest iridescent
Full
Moon
Encircled with mist
Glows world beneath
Crystal sparkles
Through sky windows
Glazed in snow drops
Mysterious message
Thrown by a moonbeam
Creative
Power
Written with diamonds
On world below

GOLDEN SCARAB

Did you send
A golden scarab
Last
Night
In my dream
Twice flew into my room
A golden message
A scarab
With wings
Large - loving
Deep golden
Did you remember
The night we
Danced
In Mexico City
Was I your golden scarab flying
Am I still
Your golden
Scarab
Silent - beautiful
Golden scarab

HAPPINESS

You are here

Secrets revealed

Where once a heavy

Heart

Where once clouded memories

Edged moments

Of joy

Where

Once

Uncertainty of knowing

Held creativity

At bay

Winds cleared dark sky

Moving

Fast

In November

Suspicion abating

Clarity progressing

Leaves falling

Away

Revealing truths

Happiness

HEAT WAVE

June, 2005

Heat is something I do not deal with very
Well
It breaks creative spell
Muses are sweating
Cats are
Fretting
Plants are wilting
Air conditioners pumping
Smog cloying
Advisories
Broadcasting
For the hard of breathing
Sidewalks are steaming
Hoses are
Spurting
Construction continues
Roofers are roofing
Hammers are
Pounding
Saws are screaming
Tires are softening
Sawdust is flying
Smog
Persisting
Dog's tongues are lolling
Raccoons are swimming
Clogging fountains

Beer
Cans clanging
Bottles jangling
Bees buzzing
Flys swarming
Rooftops
Burning
Hurricanes forming
Cottagers leaving
Traffic congesting
Neighbours
Agitating - annoying
Lakes polluting
Rivers drying
Insects
Biting
Barbecues wafting
Contractors dumping
Electricity diminishing
Brave ones
Jogging - cycling - rollerblading
Noise traveling
Nerves
Fraying
Friendships broken
Sunblock selling
Instant sun tan applying
Longing for rain
Resulting from
Hurricanes forming
Cottagers
Leaving
Traffic congesting

Neighbours agitating - complaining -
Negating
Lakes polluting
Rivers drying
Insects biting
Friendships broken
Contractors
Dumping
Barbecues wafting
Electricity diminishing
Brave ones jogging -
Cycling - rollerblading
Noise traveling
Nerves fraying
Sunblock
Selling
Instant suntan applying
Umbrellas appearing
Longing for rain
Resulting
From
Heat wave

HOISTING COLOURS

Invitation to the
Painter
Represent your country
In The Florence Biennale
The colours had been
Hoisted
On the personal website
Of a Canadian
Lifer artist
Chosen by a
Jury
As a likely Canadian painter
To be honoured in this way
In Canada
Barely known
Amongst the many artists
Dealers - population
Recognition from
A cultured country
Was worth every effort
Work - expense
To hoist our
Colours
Amidst the many flags - many nations
The artist's triumph
The
Recognition
Would be within her heart
A private - solitary -

Celebration
The joy of a life
Sacrificed to art
To hoisting Canadian colours
In a foreign abroad -
Broad
Cultured land
She painted our energy
Accomplishments
Sung and
Unsung heroes
Of this vast Canadian homeland
Who had touched her
Life
Briefly - willingly - separately
Allowing her
The
Hoisting
Of Colours

HOTTEST SUMMER IN MEMORY

Power Failure

July

26, 2005

Hot humid - rain - dark

Toronto - city centre

Rosedale south

The

Victorian enclave

Named Cabbagetown

Houses joined in a row

Built in

1886

Named Pine Terrace

On Sackville Street

Dark

Shops on Parliament

Street

Dark

Employees standing outside

Worried expressions

On their heat

Stressed faces

Glowing with sweat

Restaraunts - pubs - closed

Business

Lost

Security down

Traffic lights down

Traffic chaos

Two days before Canada

Day

Trying to stock up

Lost without power

Computer communication

Down

Cell phone battery needs charging

Emergency calls limited

Food in

Frig melting

Nineteen hours of misery

When will it end?

Then

Looked

Through window

To see the fountain

In my little garden pond

Dancing -

Singing again

Which we shall take for granted again

Until we receive our

Hydro bills

Communication restored again

After

The Hottest Summer In

Memory

INSTINCT OF WARNING

Volcanic eruption

Whispered in my

Ear

Danger said the voice

Nose smelled the smoke

Warning

Feet began to

Move

Warning

Danger vibrating in blood

Instinct rushed through

Brain

Run - run - run

Before molten lava flows

Instinct of warning

LIVE

Can we live without each other

Can we live in this field

Of poppies

Without each other

How much must we prove

That we cannot

Live

Without each other

Our destined love

We cannot deny

Confess

Our

Mistakes

Confess

Our longing

Tell our deepest love

For the mystical

Legacy

Confess

What is hidden in our hearts

It is love

It is need

It is

giving

It is youth

It is live

MILLENNIUM STOVE

Sits upon slate
Pedestal
Forrest racer green
Colour borrowed from Jaguar
Small elegant
Cast iron
Slender curved legs
Raise lovely form
Red pot rests - bubbling
- Cooking
Black pipe protrudes
Spreading heat - aroma of wood
Burning
In my Cabbagetown kitchen
Fire roars inside windowed door
Calming
Warming
Comforting heat
A true friend indeed
Which greets me
On chilly
Mornings
Afternoons evenings
While I write
At the round marble table
Near to
My
Millennium Stove

MUSIC IS POETRY IS PAINTING

Tentative
Fingers
Placed on the instrument
Keys - strings - bow
Lips placed on
Mouthpiece
Feet placed on pedals
Percussion hammers on
Drums
Wind
Strings
Expressing the scene
On our emotions
Placing new - remembered
Longings
Placing
Us
In it's spell
Penetrating our lives
Living - past - future
Floating
Us on the rivers
Of our individuality
Realizing
Music is poetry is
Painting
Through sun dappled gardens - rooftops
Singing fountains
Traffic
Congested roads
Row houses - thoughts emanate
Through connecting
Beams

MY CANADIAN ICONS

Those who have influenced my

Life

Not always free from strife

Canadian Diamonds each one

Untainted

By violence - but hard won

Connections so mystical - mysterious

I

Painted until I was almost delirious

Standing at my easel through sunshine

And storm

For a year and three months until I was worn

Preparing for

The Florence Bienniale

To which I had been invited as a Canadian

Perennale

Showing the world what Canadians are made of

Was my mission -

Instilled ambition to speak of

Some of my subjects who understood art

Allowed

Me to paint freely expressing my part

As a chronicler of lives lived to

This point

Others became rigid - frigid with fright

Seeing themselves

In a different light

Those who have influenced my life

All diamonds

Were joined together - like it or not
Formed a spectacular display on the
Spot

1.

Ronald Venter hung at the top
Having drilled each canvas
And screwed to stay
With his expertise - noble engineering his
Way

2.

Margaret McMillan of world fame
For writing the book Paris 1919 - the
Game
Hung below and to the left
Wearing a shawl of fine weft

3.

Our Lady
Of Dreams hung to the right
With her cat Frigga in plain
Sight
Surrounded by a young lover's photos of life

4.

Sr. Eduardo Robson hung to her
Right
A distinguished man with financial might
Latin America's gift to
Merrill Lynch

A visit to Mexico made painting his portrait a
Cinch

5.

Hung in the middle is renowned historian
Professor Emeritus Trevor O.
Lloyd
An Oxford education filling the void
Smiling shyly under gothic
Window's heaven

6.

The lawyer George Rust De Eye
Hung below to the left
Holding
His book of Toronto's antiquarians
Dressed in his robe recognized round
The globe

7.

Liz Wylie, good friend at U of Toronto's Art Centre
Her
Curatorial expertise imaged in mediaevel's gallery
Was the first Icon
To sit for one hour
As calm as a flower

8.

Cherry Carnon the realtor
Hung next on the left
With St. George's award winning medal

For
Proving her metal

9.

Finally the bottom spot
Was taken by Richard T. La
Prairie
Of diamond miner's Darnley Bay
His home town's symbol of Timmins
On display
After much red tape and delay
My Canadian Icons arrived
Safely I must say
In Florence, Italy and hung on display
In the Fortessa
Di Basso surrounded by a mote
I was proud and given space to gloat
The
Highlight of my career held dear
Came with the eminent Dr. John T.
Spike
In critique of my work - which he liked!
I had climbed a diamond
Shaped mountain
Pulled us all up to the peak
Without slipping or sliding
Or hiding
From the international world of art
Which tends to set us
Apart
I had run Seabiscuit's race

Without loosing my pace
My Canadian
Icons can now save face
With world recognition in this time and space

MY LITTLE RED BOOK OF POETRY

It is slim and
Bright red
A gold Celtic knot adorns its bed
My first book of poetry
A
Lifetime of thought
Which the enlightened have bought
It is slim and
Bright red
My little red book of poetry
I see it at airports
Tucked under
Arms
Waiting to reveal its amazing charms
I see it at bus stops
While
Waiting to board
Eager eyes devour it
Cover to cover - oh lord!
It is
My first book of poetry
I see it on ships
A sailor's anchor
Back to
Real world
A dreamer's destination
Put into words
It is my little red book
Of poetry

I see it on streetcars

Being read through lights

Standing up -

Sitting down

Some are dog-eared and worn

Have been carried through storms

I

See it in restaurants

Beside foie gras and Shiraz

Somewhat stained with

Drippings of nectar of gods

My little red book of poetry

I see it in

Mexico

At posh resorts

Touched with sun - oil and sand

Still holding

It's own

Not for the bland

My little red book of poetry

I see it in

Rome

Under the dome

Where priests roam

Standing out in the light

Under

Darkness of night

My little red book of poetry

I

See it in Scotland

All shiny and bright

Being held by the

Grander

Published by Zander

The poet's white knight

I see it on cruise ships

Beside

Deck chairs

Waiting to be picked up

By the wealthy while they eat up

My

Little red book of poetry

I see it in India

The Punjab for sure

Being

Read in Sanskrit's allure

My little red book of poetry

Which I have

Writ

I see it borrowed

From library stacks

Before it becomes

Faded

Displayed on voluminous racks

My little red book of poetry

I see it circling

The globe

Around and around

Over and over again

Even on a space

Probe

Reprinted in millions of tomes

I see it in every language to be found

On

The global round

And I will be very pleased
And oh so rich from the
Sales
Of my little red book of poetry

OUR SONG

January 19, 2006

The e-mailed music
Long
Distance phone call
The closeness
Of lovers held apart by the
Years
Making love
With music
She with the poetry
She wrote for him
He with his
Love of music
He sent to her
They listened together breathless
Long
Distance
Tears of sadness
Tears of joy
Tears of longing
Tears of the
Past
Tears for the present
Tears for the future
This precious gift
This
Haunting music
As it caressed
Their hearts
Their souls
Making music of
Love together
Our Song

NEW YEAR'S EVE DAY 2005

It is snowing
Squirrels
Dashing about in my small green and white garden
Looking for buried
Nuts and bread
This last day of 2005 finds me grateful
Filled with
Love
For my son Andrew, daughter-in-law Renu
For my new life as a published
Poet
For new friends the sales of my book
MYSTIC WILLS
For my venture
Into the exotic world of digital prints
International exhibitions -
Sophia, Bulgaria, Tuerto, Argentina
For the annuity from the evaluation of my
House
Here on Sackville Street in Old Cabbagetown
In the city of
Toronto Ontario Canada
For the opportunities
2006 will bring
To travel to
Exotic places
For good health
For optimism
Feeling of excitement
For the
Present and future
And maybe a new love
On this
New Year's Eve Day
2005

NEW YEAR'S EVE 2005

Snow storm
Romantic
Limousine arrives on time
Chauffeur in black hat
Ushers me to car
Offering his
Arm
I am prepared to dance
The night away
As a single
Young at heart
Widow
With any moveable man
I am wearing a movable gown
Black wraparound
With slits
To reveal legs in black sheers
Black velvet pumps
Silver
Braided
Black feather boa sprinkled with silver
For up-dated look
Jet
Beaded choker and cuffs
Shiny up-do sparkled hair
Gray streak arranged
Wind blown
Antique crystal combs
Antique crystal drop earrings
Emerald
Marquisette dinner ring
To attract any moveable man
New Year's Eve
2005

NOVEMBER TWENTY THIRD 2005

First snow
Storm
Invitation
Dinner at George
Across the table
From her friend
Handsome
Historian
Masses of wild
Tousled white hair
Sparkled eyes
Beautiful Oxford
Accent
Gourmand - orders
Spectacular food - wine
Pulled rabbit
Confeit
Other small portions
Exotic names
After on the street
Snow falling
Gently
Waiting for taxi
He held her strongly - closely
Kissed her again and
Again
Ignoring passersby - customers leaving George
Happy - lovely way
To celebrate
First snow storm

ODE TO MY FINANCIAL ADVISOR

A Valentine for: F.

Stephen Ford

If you can't love your Financial Advisor

Who can you

Love?

Whose heart is larger than your investment?

Your Financial

Advisor

Who will bring a bouquet of flowers to your first book launch?

Who will

Fix your dilapidated fence?

Who will offer to fix the leak in your

Roof?

Who will share his plumber - to fix the flood?

Your Financial

Advisor

Who will arrange for your reverse mortgage - annuity?

Who will be

With you when the appraiser arrives?

Who will stand beside you when

Strangers arrive?

Who will advise you on life's difficult decisions?

Who will

Calm your fears?

Your Financial Advisor

Who can you trust

Implicitly?

Who really cares about your life?

Who can you confidently confide in -

As a true friend?
That is why I love
My Financial Advisor

PAINTING IS POETRY

Rhythm of movement
Rhythm of
Brush strokes
Rhythm of choosing colors
Composition - subject -
Style
Rhythm of the soul
Set Free
To move
To explore
To express
Deepest
Emotions
Technique learned
Technique forgotten
Rhythm of flowing
Of
Emotion
The rhythm of river
Of thoughts
Submerged
Surfacing
In the painting
The
Sweep of thought
Surging up from unconscious
Sweep of hand
Across a
Canvas - a page
Realizing
Painting is poetry

PEARL MOON

Pearl moon
Full in the
Sky
Traveling through seas of clouds
Your face smiling - mouth moving
Directly
Above this city sleeping
Dreaming
What message do you impart
To us
Tonight?
Does my lover see you tonight?
Does he hear your message?
Relay to
Him
It is love
In his far distant land
Pearl moon
Full in the sky
Does he
Dream
Words I wish to hear?
Words I wish to say?
Connect our
Souls
Pearl moon
Full in the sky
My companion eternal
Pearl moon
Full in the
Sky

POLO PRINCE

I see you as a youth
Riding your polo
Pony
Proud smiling
Feeling your pony
Responding to your wish
Mexican
Boots
Perfectly fitted
In glistening stirrups
Guiding your pony
Through
Desert cactus
Under mountains - volcanic shadows
Lush fields
High walled
Gardens
Cascading bougainvillea
Warm sun
Gentle rain
Gaucho hat tied
Beneath your chin
Blue eyes scanning
Tall trees - verdant green
Your
playing field
All eyes turned to watch
The lusty - luscious trail of
My
Beautiful
Polo Prince

RED FIRE DOG

Oh red fire dog
Faithful
Companion
Loyal Friend
Loving protector
Be all of these
To me and my family
In
This your year 2006
Bring peace and joy
Oh blazing red fire dog
Let us
Be freed
From war - Chaos
Let us be creative - prosperous
Brightly
Blazing
Red fire dog of the east
Make dreams of love
Come true
Let us run
Free in your light
Beautiful brightly blazing
Red Fire Dog

RED! RED! RED!

Request - write a poem about
Your favourite colour
Is it the colour of my magic bed?
Is it deep
Indigo blue of the sky at night?
Is it the rich purple of a pashima
Shawl
Violet of dioxazine hue?
Racer green of of the convertible
1958 Jaguar
XKE?
Is it phthalo blue deepening the sky and sea?
Iridescent gold of the
Sun and kings?
Golden eye of the shapeshifter Egypts Horace?
Iridescent
Silver of the moon in fullness?
Hunter green found in clan
Tartans?
Forrest green in my wild green garden of healing?
Maybe it is turquoise
Sometimes
Maybe manganese blue lightly applied
Deep velvet red of the
Mexican sombrero
Hanging on my studio wall ?
Gift from an old lover
Today
At this moment

It is Red! Red! Red!

Colour of blood coursing through

Our veins

Life giving force

Colour of vitality - power - of base

Chackra

At the base of our spine

Today it is mine

Red! Red! Red!

SACHERTORTE

Delivered by her long lost
Handsome son
Andrew
Her amazing beautiful boy
Brilliant painter - illustrator - poet -
Singer - composer
Carried carefully
Flown across the sea
From its home
In Vienna, Austria
Lovely pale wooden box
With little gold
Lock
Sachertorte, Austria
Burned into the lid
Contained
Two small chocolate topped
Cakes
For her birthday
She would never forget
That lovely warm evening
In June
Under yellow striped awning
On the patio at Provence, on Amelia
Street
In Old Cabbagetown
The laughter they shared
The gifts of
Closeness - knowing - learning
The delicate richness
Of
Sachertorte

SINGING SANDS

Listen......
Can you hear the
Singing sands
Humming
Ticking, tocking, talking
Humming
Singing sands
Time
Has composed your song
Singing from your grains of glass
Resonating your
Song
Singing sands
Your dunes shifting, sifting, sliding
Back and
Forth
Gulls, sandpipers, fish, ships hear your
Singing sands
Your song of
Picnics past
Of lover's joyous laughter
Childhood castles
Of
Lover's
Crystal goblets half filled
Can you hear the singing sands
Waving to and
Fro
Ticking, tocking, talking
Humming
Warm breezes carry your
Song
Singing sands
I can hear you

SNOW

Keep falling lovely snow
Make my garden
Glisten
Make my footprints fly
Make dreamers
Dream
Romantically
Fondly
Adventurously
Admiringly
Voluptuously
Vibrantly
Make trees bow - bend
As
I pass by
Laughingly
Make a grand coat
Of frothy white
To cover with
Love
My garden urns - benches
Cast a winter spell
Soften our visible
World
With clean whiteness
Keep falling
Lovely snow

SONG OF LOVE

I fly to you
On wings of love
On
Wings of memory
On wings of silver
On wings of music
I hear in my
Soul
You sent to me
On wings of our song
Through silent stars
On beams of
Moonlight
Connecting our love
I see you
Feel you
I long for your touch
I
Am a bird
Feed me
As I land on your hand
On wings of love
On wings of
Our love song

SPANISH LOVE SONG

Guitars
Harmonicas
Strumming
Flutes
Twirling us into our dance
Our bodies
Entwined
Moving
Flowing
Ripples
On a wave
To and fro
Letting us flow
We do not know where
Do not
Care to know
Or if it will end
Wash over us
In rapture
Look
Deeply
Into
Our eyes
Our souls
As one body
One intertwined thought
Float us
Away
Our destiny
Our Spanish love song

SPINNING - WEAVING - SPINNING

The small
World
Isolated world
World of a widow
In a community of families
Living alone
In the
Eleven roomed - tall - narrow Victorian house
Filled with her
Art and an art collection
Anchoring the south end
Of a connected row of
Victorian houses
Built in 1886
Yellow fire hydrant outside
In the city
Centre
Called Cabbagetown
A row of well-meaning
Family oriented
Folks
Professors - lawyers - financial experts - theatrical types - artists
The
Others - eccentrics
As far as she could glean
From the on-going
Gossip
Freely given
From those whose vibrations
Worked north and south
Of the
Centre
She herself would be included

In the gossip
Probably as an
Eccentric
Who does not fit in
To the pretend world
The "we control the
Street and the world"
She controlled her own freedom-filled world
Author - poet - painter
No dog or young children - but a cultured cat
Companion
Life filled her small wild green garden
On the other side of
The tall fence
Where her enviable private parking space
Housed her
1990 red Subaru Legacy with two flat tires
Miracles happened to her -
Quite frequently
Old lovers found her - old friends found her - family
Found her
She had love - joy - in her heart
She was out of the
Loop
Foreign countries requested her paintings - prints and poetry
Miracles
Happened to her - frequently
She was a widow and a mother - found
Spinning
- weaving - spinning
A new life of freedom - research - exploration -
Learning
Spinning with golden threads of love
Production -
Creativity
Spinning - weaving - spinning
Bliss

SUBLIME CONNECTION

Fate once again
Introduces
Sublime connection
A stranger - another stranger
Led the thread of
Ariadne to
Once-upon-a-time work-place friends
Thought lost in world of
Television and film
Reappear to meet again
Friends known
Centuries
Ago
Reunion arranged
Four Seasons Hotel
Joy, laughter
Sharing tales
Wonder
Awe
Filling gaps
Quaffs of shiraz
Ups and downs
Progress -
Successes
Blessings
I give thanks for the miracle
Sublime Connection

TERPSICHOREAN TALENT

Or...the art of
Dancing
Should have a sense of rhythm
Should have good legs
But who would have
Thought
It is not your two legs
But your two terpsichorean genes
Which
Make your dancing steps
As light as a feather on the breeze
So....come
Dance with me
I have the terpsichorean genes
Feel your two genes
Revving
Working your two legs flying
Come dance with me
Salsa, mamba, waltz,
Two stepping
Charleston, move to the rhythm
Tapping, flamenco, tango,
Minuet
Watch your two genes working your
Two legs flying
Exercise your two
Genes
With your terpsichorean talent
Come dance with me

MAPS

It is said if you draw a map
Of everywhere you
Have been
You draw your fate
Can this be true
Shall I dare to draw
The
Map
Can I remember everywhere
I have been
What is the next point
On the
Map
The map of my fate
Dare to draw
Foretell my fate
Is it a
Circle
Surrounding me
Forward - foreword
Until it is return - return
A mandala
To
The centre
Of the starting point
Of the map
Of my fate
Draw

TOMORROWS

With tomorrows
Each celebration
Nitual
Promises to love
Where thoughts
With
Laughter
Song
Sunshine
Grace
Flowers
Fragrance
Blossoms into bliss
Turning dreams
To awe and wonder

REMOTE TASTE OF DANFORTH

August 7, 2005

Now
With grateful feet
Dipped into dancing fountain pool
Cooled from
Afternoon's heat
Music drifts through
Multicultural celebrations
The
Danforth's Taste
Across Bloor Street viaduct
Down Dawn Valley's Don
River
Reaching Cabbagetown's small wild garden
On Sackville Street
Rhythms of
songs Greek
Mingled with aromas Greek
East Indian, Far Eastern
Imaginings
Of crowded streets
Crowded sidewalk cafes
Happily served food and
Drink
Belly dancers
Maneuvering - clicking - clanging
Teasing the shy
Coins
Tossing - hips swaying
Engulfed the small wild garden
In Cabbagetown
On
Sackville Street

TRAIN HOUSE

My house is a train
Enter front or
Back doors
Compartments on either side
Long hallway connecting
One can
Hear the refrain
Movement back and forth
Along the line of rails
Foot
Steps to and fro
Railings to observations light
To watch the seasons go
By
While moving back and forth
Along the line of rails
To view
Changes as we progress
Through each luxurious coach
Here an art gallery or
Two and more
Entering through compartments
Caboose at end
Holds warm
Fire in stove
Looks out into gardens changes
Riding the rails of my
Train house

VIEW FROM CABBAGETOWN

First snow
Storm
Winter is here
No longer making us guess
How much longer we can put
Off
Preparation
Snow shovels ready ice scrapers at hand
Stored wood
Inside
To burn in stove
Wind howls through narrow streets
Cracks - crevices -
Doors - windows
Victorian houses stand tall
In Cabbagetown
Holding on -
Weathering blasts
Snow flying - blinding walking
Icy - slippery - slow
Footing
LED lights glowing festive
Cars driving slowly cautiously
Home
Late for dinner
Bay street invisible
Through whipping snow
I view
Safely warmly inside
Third floor arrow shaped window
My panoramic viewing of
first snow storm - window
In Cabbagetown

VISITOR

The intrusive visitor
Confirmed
My
Choice to live alone
In beauty - peace - joy
Freedom to be myself
To
Paint
To write
To compose on the baby grand piano
To explore without
Negativity
Without envy
Intrusion
Demands on time
Private
Thoughts
Meditation
Freedom
To enjoy
Friends
I choose to be with
The visitor
Seemed
Frantic
Desperate
To move into
My world
I am glad of this illuminating -
Confirming visitor

MISTLETOE DREAM

In this powerful dream
Two
Mistletoe wreaths were presented to me
At my front door
To hang on your
Front doors
Exquisitely beautifully fragrant
Thick - rich - shiny -
Smooth
Deep green foliage
Clusters of white berries throughout
Resembling
Moon flowers
What message is this?
Is it from my Viking ancestor's
Belief
That mistletoe has the power
To raise humans from the dead?
Relating
To the resurrection of Balder
God of summer and sun?
Is it from Frigga
- Balder's mother
Goddess of love and beauty
Who kissed air - fire -
Water - earth
For the joy of having her son Balder
Returned to life?
Are

My doors adorned with mistletoe wreaths

In place of laurel

Wreaths?

Have I passed a test? If so what test?

Or is it from my Druid

Ancestors

Telling me they are performing miracles

With mistletoe healing -

Fertility - protection from witchcraft?

Had a spell been cast over me?

Has the

Spell been neutralized

By the gifts of mistletoe wreaths?

Have I been

Brought back to life today?

Am I fertile again?

Am I healed from

Something I did not recognize?

Am I protected once more?

Oh Frigga goddess of

Love and beauty

Thank you for your tears

Turning mistletoe red berries

To white

To new life - new growth

To returning my son to me

THE TALE OF THE VINEGAR HILL CREW

Planned and

Designed as a Christmas surprise

For the TVOntario studio crew to

Rise

Who chose me as one they would work with

In permanence - with no

Disguise

I began with excited delight

While teaching scheduling officer

Reolph

De Jonge how not to go wrong

To paint this amazing sight

18 men

Standing up in a boat

Symbolizing our studio afloat

Led lined to keep it

Quiet

From the shaking of the subway moat

Reolph sat at the stern

Singing

And playing his guitar to learn

Preparing for his Young and Wild -

Redhill Road

Guitar band of this land

Wearing an anchor round his ankle

To

Steady the boat from drifting in an award angle

Three women sat at the

Bow

Susan Beaven - Mar Budd and shy - trembling little me

With

Appropriate headdresses attached to our hair for all to see

Indicating lives we

Would rather be living and giving

Now we were a motley crew

Who worked

The productions

To be aired

Educating the enlightened and unwashed

Few

We were broadcast technicians and some musicians

My immediate

Thought

Was to make us look smart

A challenge for the skills of art

So there we

Were all dressed in white

Borrowed from a laboratory site

The gentlemen

- Loosely called -

Wore a variety of shapes of head gear

From captain's

Hats - bowlers - an outback and a top hat

All in black my dears

Could

Not see their feet so no spats

Crew Leader John Meadows

Rode his white

Stallion above our heads -

Galloping on the red brick road in front of

Our abode

Our white knight ready for flight day or night
One Tom
Savage flew in a balloon
Over the building close to the moon
Charging ten
Cents a ride
To satisfy his pride
At Yonge and Eglinton
Our home for the
Duration as long as we made our donation
Our exalted union leader - one
Shawn Ryerson
Not a shy person
Flying our banner for some
Recognition
Stood riding his deer with absolutely no fear
Now this strongly talented
Srew
Hold objects for which they are bound
To paychecks which seem far
And few
Mortgages - a lover's little black book - house building tools
-
A racing flag - painting pallets - boats - barbells - poetry books
A
Black dog is there too - a bike - birds on shoulders
Whispering
Inspiration - a much needed libation
On the left cynics and doubters -
Pointing to
The optimists on the right - swaying and waving
Their upright
Arms form the sails of our boat

Our war canoe set to float

On the roof of

The grand building of TVO

Is a wise - old snowy owl amused by this

Scene

Expresses himself in a very loud hoot!

And that is

The Tail Of The

Vinegar Hill Crew

Thank you

Which I painted in my studio

On Vinegar

Hill

Known only to a few

Where once stood an ancient still

Which made an

Intoxicating brew

Turned into vinegar

Revenge overtook the enraged

Populous

Under darkness of night

They then rolled the barrels down the hill

- Crashed and flipped

Into the Rouge river

Which became Vinegar

Dip

Because of my paintings title

Signs were then erected by the Town of

Markham

Indicating Vinegar Hill

VENUS

Good morning Venus
Sparkling brightest
In
Pre dawn sky
Shine on me
Lend me your many facetted diamond
Shimmer me
With your magnetism
Let me glow with love
Shower me with eternal beauty
Here on earth
Under your spell
Glimmer me with your wisdom
From the
Beginning of time
Notice me
You are my ruling planet
I was born in your
Glow
A long time ago
Reflect in me
Good morning
Venus
Sparkling
Brightest
In pre dawn sky

MULBERRY TREE

July 1, 2005
Canada Day
Ladened with sweet dark
Berries
The mulberry tree of great stature
Rains on me its rich fruit
As I read
In my small shaded garden
Dappled in sunlight
Fountain in the oval
Shaped pond singing
Celebration song
Echoing, circling this lovely secret
Garden
Wind happy waiving branches
Of the mulberry tree
Which bestows
Its berries on me
Landing on my sun hat
Bouncing on my white
Blouse
Leaving deep red stain
In satisfaction of landing
I say thank you
And eat
Them
Savouring each succulent gift
From the mulberry tree
The wind

Increases in its humour
Now throwing berries at me
In my Argentinean red
Wine
As if to enrich its magic
On my bare thighs
On my calves
At my
Toes
In my hair
In my sandals
On my green lounge
Whipping across the brick
Floor of the garden
Dancing - rolling jumping
Closer to the pond
In the
Cast iron urns
Dropping on geranium leaves soft beds
In the hydrangea
Bush
In the box wood bush
In the cedar trees
Locus tree
Imbedding in the
Muscoka chairs
Victorian benches
New black shiny squirrels
Cleaning
Garden path
Bombing target
Frigga cat oblivious
Sleeping in vines - rose

Leaves
Pounding on the fence
Ants scrambling
To enjoy the smashed
Spoils
Butterflies swooping
To catch the action
Messaging the
Celebration
Gifts of the mulberry tree
Playfully eyeing
Weeping spruce by the
Pond
Darting arrows
As its warriors soft green waving shields
Diverting
Berries into sparkling pond
For a summer swim - sail
Boat ride
On bubbling
Waves
My companion
Canada Day celebration
In the garden of
The Mulberry
Tree

www.ingramcontent.com/pod-product-compliance
Lightning Source LLC
LaVergne TN
LVHW091728190726
843493LV00001B/498